The Bad Word Book

Etymology, Definitions, & Usage

By

Karen Vieira

The Bad Word Book

Etymology, Definitions, & Usage

By

Karen Vieira

The Bad Word Book: Etymology, Definitions, & Usage

By Karen Vieira

Copyright © June 2017
Alpharetta, Georgia

All rights Reserved. No part of this book may be reproduced or transmitted in any form by any means, electronic or mechanical, including photocopying and recording, or by any information storage and retrieval system, except as may be expressly permitted by the 1976 Copyright Act or in writing from the publisher.

Introduction

$%&#! Say it! It feels good doesn't it? That's because profanity has been known to have a cathartic effect on users. As a matter of fact, cussing, cursing, swearing, blaspheming, or whatever you call it, has several benefits beyond just making you feel great. It can relieve pain, make you laugh, help you make friends, get vengeance without violence, and gain power during a conversation.

Profanity or 'swear' words, date back to the Romans according to literature expert Melissa Mohr, but could go back even earlier. Certain words and phrases were not to be said in the temple and as time went on, the bible warns against the profane as well; hence the terms 'swearing' and 'cursing.'

It's crazy to think about the mere utterance of organized grunts can not only have the positive impacts mentioned above, but can get you in quite a lot of trouble as well; it's best to steer clear of a few unless you like losing teeth.

This book can be used as a reference on the etymology of some of the major expletives, or a thesaurus for ethnic slurs and body parts, or just a way to get a laugh while taking a shit.

Remember, words can hurt, so let this be a warning:

SAYING SOME OF THESE WORDS MAY GET YOU KILLED!

That said, have a good laugh and enjoy this mother fucking book.

Ass

N. 1. Butt
    2. Idiot
    3. Donkey

Etymology- *It comes from the early Germanic word 'ars', which meant buttocks or rump.*

Ex.1. Look at the **ass** on that Greta.

Ex.2. Tyrone is an **ass** for wearing bowling shoes to the track meet.

Ex.3. Our family rode **asses** into the Grand Canyon.

Combinations- Ass can be combined with an unlimited number of words to add humorous variations. Ex. Asshat, Asscock, Assfuck and Assmuncher.

Bastard

N. 1. An illegitimate child
    2. A jerk or rascal
    3. One deserving pity

Etymology-*Bastard is from the Late Latin term 'bastardus' and Old French 'bastard' for illegitimate child. It wasn't considered vulgar until the early 19th century.*

Ex.1. The man left his pregnant wife, so now she will have to raise a **bastard**.

Ex.2. Hey, stop that **bastard**, he stole my wallet!

Ex.3. The poor **bastard** never stood a chance.

Bitch

N. 1. Female Dog
    2. Unpleasant woman
V. 1. To complain

Etymology-*Bitch most likely comes from Germanic origins and from Old English as 'Bicce', meaning female canine.*

Ex.1. Someone needs to teach that bitch to sit.

Ex.2. Marge took the last piece of chocolate, what a bitch.

Ex.1 Lance bitched for an hour about his bad haircut.

Combinations- 'Son of a Bitch' is a hugely popular form of insult dating back to the early 18th century in this form, and even earlier in different terms with similar meaning

Cock

N. 1. Rooster
    2. Penis

Etymology- *It is from Old English as 'cocc', which meant male bird. It dates back to the early 17th century in its penis meaning.*

Ex.1. That cock sure likes to strut his stuff.

Ex2. Jeannette bellowed with joy as she gripped the over-sized cock of her lover.

Combinations- There are numerous variations like cock fag, cock tease, cock master, cock chugger, cock sucker, cock mongler, cockadoodlefuck, cock shitter, cock dick

Cunt

N. 1. Vagina
2. Most offensive term for a woman

Etymology- *Early Germanic word and related to the Norse word 'kunta'. Latin for vulva is cunnus, but its modern meaning dates back to the early 14th century Middle English*

Ex.1. Reggie inserted his throbmonster into her cunt.

Ex.2. Shit, that bitch is a cunt!

Combinations- Cunt nose, cunt face, cunt whore, cunt fuck, ass cunt

Damn

V. 1. To condemn
Adj.1. Emphasis of frustration
Exc.1. Expresses anger or surprise

Etymology-*Origins go back to the word 'damner' during the late 1300s in Old French, meaning 'to condemn'*

Ex.1. Damn you to hell!

Ex.2. Give me the damn bottle!

Ex.3. Damn! I just stubbed my fucking toe.

Combinations- Damn it, Goddamn, Hot damn, Damn right/straight, I don't give a damn

Dick

N. 1. Penis
    2. A jerk

Etymology- *It has been used to describe a jerk since at least the 17th century, and was used by British soldiers in the late 19th century as another word for penis.*

Ex.1. Gerald knew his weiner was too small to satisfy Rhonda.

Ex.2. That dick cut me off!

Combinations- Dick head, Dick bitch, Little Dicky, Dick fuck

Dyke

N. 1. Lesbian
    2. A masculine woman

Etymology- *Dyke's early usage actually comes from the verb 'bulldyking' (lesbian sex) and was used by African Americans in the early 20th century.*

Ex.1. Did you hear that Miranda is a dyke?

Ex.2. That dyke just kicked Micah's ass!

Combinations- dirty dyke, butch dyke, taco eating dyke, cunt scissoring dyke

Fag

N. 1. Homosexual
    2. Cigarette (British)
    3. Effeminite man

Etymology- *American in origin for homosexual, dating back to the early 20th century. Also use to describe a disdainful woman dating back several hundred years.*

Ex.1. Lance does ballet and takes it in the butt, what a fag...

Ex.2. Can I bum a fag, homo!

Ex. 3. That fag walks like a woman.

Combinations- Cock fag, Fag Fuck, Butt-fucking faggot, ass fag, fag mouth

Fuck

N. 1. Offensive term for a jerk
V. 1. To have sex
Exc. 1. Term of frustration

Etymology-*Dates back to the early 16th century. It has been outlawed in print during the 1800s in Britain and America due to obscenity laws. It has its roots in Germanic, meaning 'to strike'.*

Ex.1. That fuck took my seat.

Ex.2. Timmy sure would like to fuck Shaniqwa.

Ex.4. Fuck! I chopped off my finger!

Combinations- Fuck head, Mother Fucker, Fuck-face, dumb-fuck, pig-fucker, and Shit-fuck

Hell

N.   1. Where the devil lives
Exc.1. Expression of displeasure

Etymology- *Origin is Germanic for 'concealed place' or 'underworld'. Other uses of the word, like 'for the hell of it' and 'hell of a' dates back to the early 20th century. Shakespeare or others in that time finds the first use of 'go to hell'*

Ex.1. You can rot in hell you son of a bitch! lol

Ex.2. What the hell just happened!?

Combinations- What the hell, hell or highwater, hell of a time, hell if I know, go to hell

Pussy

N. 1. Vagina
    2. Coward or weak

Etymology-*Could be from the Old Norse for 'pouch' or from the term for a cat, which dates to the early 18th century.*

Ex.1. Brian slapped his wang on that pussy.

Ex.2. Jon is such a pussy for not trying out for the football team!

Combinations- Fat Pussy, Dirty Pussy, Pussy Fag, Giant Pussy, and Pussy shit

Shit

N. 1. Feces
    2. A horrible person
V. 1. To poop
Exc.1. Exclamation of displeasure

Etymology- *A 15th century Old English word 'scitte', which meant diarrhea. Middle English 'Shitel' meant dung or turd, and most modern variants like 'give a shit', 'load of shit' and 'shit-list' are from the early 20th century.*

Ex.1. Carl left his dog's shit all over my lawn

Ex.2. Craig is a shit for not leaving a tip.

Ex.3. Lu shit his brains out after going to Mexico!

Ex.4. Shit! My boner went away!

Combinations- Shit head, Shit Fuck, Dumb Shit, Dipshit, and Shit-Dick

Slut

N. 1. An extremely promiscuous woman

Etymology- *Could be 15th century Germanic in origin with the word 'schlutt', which meant 'dirty woman'. The promiscuous meaning doesn't seem to come in to the English language until the mid-20th century.*

Ex.1. Joan is a slut because she fucked the entire baseball team, and then the football team.

Combinations- Slut bag, Slut whore, Ass-Slut, Slutty slut

Body Parts

Penis

Bologna
Boomstick
Choad
Chubby
Cock
Cum gun
Dangler
Dick
Ding dong
Doink
Dong
Flesh flute
Fuck stick
Jimmy
Johnson
Joystick
Junk
Love muscle
Love stick
Manhood

Member
One-eyed monster
Pecker
Peepee
Peter
Pocket rocket
Purple-headed warrior
Rod
Sausage
Schlong
Shaft
Tallywhacker
Third leg
Throbmonster
Tool
Trouser snake
Unit
Wang
Weewee
Wiener
Willy
Yogurt slinger

Vagina

Beef Curtains
Bearded Oyster
Beaver
Clam
Cock Socket
Coochie
Cum Bucket
Cunt
Dick Mitten
Front Butt
Fur Burger
Hair Pie
Hot Pocket
Hump Hole
Landing Pad
Meat Wallet
Muff
Pole hole
Pussy
Salami sheath

**Snatch
Twat
Vagoo
Vertical Taco**

Breasts

Balloons
Bazookas
Boobies
Coconuts
Gazongas
Honkers
Hoohas
Hooters
Jugs
Kahunas
Knockers
Mountains
Melons
Pillows
Plums
Tatas
Tetons
Titties
Utters
Yayas

Butt

Ass
Backside
Badunkadonk
Booty
Britches
Bum
Buns
Caboose
Can
Cheeks
Derriere
Dumper
Fanny
Fart Box
Fudge Factory
Full Moon
Gluteus Maximus
Heinie
Keister
Money Maker

Patootie
Pooper
Rear-end
Rectum
Rump
Shitbox
Tail
Tukhus
Tushy

Printed in Great Britain
by Amazon